Introduction

My family, fellow team members, and other friends sometimes give me a hard time. "Hey, Luis," they say with a smile, "are you going to talk about the principles of victorious Christian living *again*?" They know from experience that I long to encourage believers to learn and apply biblical principles for living triumphantly in Jesus Christ.

Yes, my passion is to win as many people as possible to Christ throughout the world. But that's only the beginning. I sincerely believe God has much more than salvation in store for each of his children. He wants us to enjoy the fact that he "always leads in triumph" every day of our lives.

I find it sad to see so many Christians who do not live victoriously in Christ. Oh, they yearn to experience the full joy he promises, but they don't know how to fill the hole in their lives. This booklet explains, in part, how to fill that void.

If you're looking for an easy three-step formula for enjoying the Christian life, please look elsewhere. Victorious Christian living can't be manufactured or masqueraded. Only God can produce it in us.

Experiencing Personal Renewal

If you were to consider the desires, motives, thoughts, and actions of most Christians, I think you would discover that every growing believer wants the same thing. New or mature, young or old, charismatic or noncharismatic, every Christian desires to live in the presence of God. Every Christian longs to communicate Jesus Christ in a powerful way. And every Christian seeks daily spiritual renewal.

As Christians, we detest any hint of stagnation in our spiritual lives. We want to know that we're growing, changing, maturing. We long for reality in our walk with God. We don't want to feel that we're stuck in the mud. We long for new, joyous experiences in the Lord—and that longing comes from the Holy Spirit.

Signs of Outer Renewal

But so often we pursue renewal in the wrong ways. When we don't enjoy daily renewal, we run from church to church, pastor to pastor, denomination to denomination, experience to experience, looking for it. We even have "renewal congresses," often held in the Holy Land. I guess people think if they can walk where Jesus walked, they'll be renewed.

People also talk to me about renewal in their churches. "Oh," they say, "our minister doesn't preach from the pulpit anymore. He wears a lapel mike and talks while he walks among the congregation. And we don't sit in rows anymore. We sit together in a big circle. It's wonderful."

If that's all spiritual renewal is, then my family experiences a renewal every spring when my wife rearranges the living room furniture. My sons and I like to keep things as they are, but Pat loves change. I like my reading chair to be in a familiar spot. I don't care whether it fits in with the surroundings or is color coordinated. I don't care about the carpeting or the plants around it. But Pat loves renewal, and every spring our house is renewed.

Moving church furniture around may symbolize renewal, but it isn't what spiritual renewal is all about. Some people believe that a lot of noise and outward change means renewal. These outward signs sometimes indicate renewal, but more often than not they're just a religious facade.

The kind of renewal we desperately long for cannot be found in a uniquely shaped building, in a different furniture arrangement, or in a more creative form of worship. The spiritual renewal we seek must come from the life of Jesus working in us and flowing through us day after day. Spiritual renewal is the evidence of Jesus Christ's work in our lives.

Key to Inner Renewal

If the spiritual renewal we long for is a result of the life of Jesus at work within us, how can this life be appropriated? The answer is found in the following verses:

> But we have this treasure in jars of clay to show that this all-surpassing power is from God and not from us. We are hard pressed on every side, but not crushed; perplexed, but not in despair; persecuted, but not abandoned; struck down, but not destroyed. We always carry around in our body the death of Jesus, so that the life of Jesus may also be revealed in our body. For we who are alive are always being given over to death for Jesus' sake, so that his life may be revealed in our mortal body. So then, death is at work in us, but life is at work in you (2 Cor. 4:7-12).

We Christians have a treasure within us . . . nothing less than God himself! No matter who we are—grandfathers, students, factory workers, housewives, business executives—no matter what we look like, God has come to indwell us, making our bodies temples of the Holy Spirit.

This truth is the heart of the gospel. Of course, Jesus' death and resurrection are the foundation of the gospel; but the heart of the gospel is that God himself indwells us. God isn't out there in orbit with the satellites. He is within us. The Bible says that when we are joined to the Lord, we become one in spirit with him (1 Cor. 6:17). Spiritual renewal is the result of the crucified and resurrected Christ living within us.

Paul says this marvelous treasure is contained in clay jars—our bodies. The Bible says that our bodies were made from the earth. When we die, our bodies go back into the earth and disintegrate to become part of nature once again. Yet God has chosen to dwell within our humble, imperfect human bodies.

Our bodies are so fragile. We have to treat them with great care. We have to feed them, wash them, clothe them, protect them. If we neglect our bodies for even a few days, they begin to show our earthly beginnings all too quickly!

A few years ago I realized just how fragile our bodies are. I noticed five spots on my face and asked a dermatologist to look at them. He examined them and said, "These are precancerous. We'd better burn them off." So he burned them off and that was the end of the problem for a time. But then I started thinking: *Today I had spots burned off. Tomorrow, some other part of me will need attention.*

Even though I exercise regularly and try to eat nutritious food, my body isn't such a great piece of equipment. No matter how hard I work to keep my jar of clay in shape, one day it will fall apart. But no matter how unimpressive our earthly bodies are, God has chosen to be the treasure within us. In our bodies dwell the power and the glory of the resurrected Christ.

Many believers accept this concept intellectually, but live as though God were up in heaven somewhere. They hustle around trying to do their best for God, never realizing that Christ lives within them. They never come to grips with the reality that the eternal, living God has chosen to live within and to work through every believer. What an awesome thought! What a difference that treasure makes in a person's life!

Nevertheless, Christians are not exempt from the troubles of life. Paul states that the treasure of the indwelling Christ doesn't eliminate every problem (2 Cor. 4:8-9). He says that we are hard pressed, perplexed, persecuted, and struck down—just like the unbelievers around us. People cheat us. People say bad things about us. Our cars break down. Our children get sick. Friends and family members die. We have the same kinds of problems our unbelieving neighbors have, but we are not crushed by affliction because Christ lives within us.

That we are not crushed by affliction is a distinguishing mark of the Christian. We may look just like unbelievers from the outside, but inside we have the blessing of the indwelling Christ to carry us through all misfortune.

Sometimes we're perplexed and confused by life. Our friends may turn against us. We may be unable to resolve a problem at work, home, or church. Things may happen to us that we don't understand, but we are not driven to despair because Christ lives within us.

We are persecuted, too. In this country we

may not face physical persecution for the sake of Christ, but we face social persecution. We may become good friends with our neighbors, but when we begin to share the Good News with them, they may stop inviting us to their parties. But persecution isn't the end of the world. No matter who turns against us, we never will be forsaken by the indwelling Christ.

Finally, Paul says we will be struck down, but never destroyed. I suppose I shouldn't admit it, but I like to watch boxing. It reminds me of spiritual warfare. When a guy takes a hard punch and falls to the canvas, you may think he's been knocked out and the match is over. But often he gets up and starts throwing punches again. That's the kind of spiritual picture Paul describes here. As Christians, we may be knocked down, but the indwelling Christ enables us to get up and go at it again.

Sustaining Inner Renewal

If the power of the living Christ is in every believer, why isn't it always visible? Why do we sometimes feel defeated, depressed, frustrated, and fruitless?

Paul explains when he says, "We always carry around in our body the death of Jesus, so that the life of Jesus may also be revealed in our body" (2 Cor. 4:10). The death of Jesus must be at work in us before we can see the results of the life of Christ. But how does the death of Jesus work in us? What does it mean in our daily lives?

It took me a long time to understand this

passage. I had decided, as every Christian must, to follow the admonition to "offer your bodies as living sacrifices, holy and pleasing to God—which is your spiritual worship" (Rom. 12:1). That decision was crucial. I had prayed, "I don't want to be a worldly Christian. I don't want to be a carnal Christian. Lord Jesus, here is my whole body, soul, and spirit. I dedicate them to you." But, like so many others, I assumed that choosing to commit myself to Christ was a one-time decision.

Two cross references to this passage also stumped me for a long time. John 12:24 refers to the grain of wheat that must fall to the ground and die before it can bear fruit, and, in Matthew 16:24, Jesus says that anyone who does not take up his cross and follow him cannot be his disciple.

No matter how many times I heard preachers speak about the grain of wheat, I didn't understand it. I didn't know how to make a hole in the ground, fall into it, and die for the Lord so I could bear fruit. And I didn't know what Jesus meant by taking up the cross.

Through further study I have come to believe that these three passages mean the same thing. Every time my will conflicts with God's will and I choose his will over mine, the death of Jesus is at work in me. When I choose God's will over my will, the grain of wheat falls to the ground and dies so that it can bear fruit. When I choose God's will over my will, I am taking up the cross of Christ.

These passages don't deal with the important

decision that an individual makes to follow Jesus, but with the future decisions every Christian must make in order to walk with the living Christ. Making that first decision to follow Christ only lays the foundation for a life-time of daily decisions to follow him.

Commitment isn't something we do once and never have to settle again. Commitment doesn't permanently eliminate conflict within our souls. We must continue to choose God's will over ours. But when we do, the Lord Jesus—who indwells us by the Holy Spirit—will work through us in dynamic ways.

In the Garden of Gethsemane, Jesus provided a perfect example of choosing God's will over our own. Jesus was the perfect man. He knew God's will for his life and wanted it. Nevertheless, Jesus wasn't a masochist who couldn't wait to be beaten and mocked, who couldn't wait for the nails to be pounded through his hands. Jesus prayed that he wouldn't have to drink such a bitter cup. But Jesus knew the will of the Father and chose God's will over his own—not in resignation, but in a clear-cut, meaningful decision.

Jesus' choice is an example to all of us. Whenever we choose God's will over ours, the death of Jesus is at work in us. We are dying to ego, pride, passion, and desire. When we choose God's will over our own, we become Christ-conscious instead of self-conscious, and the life of Jesus begins to flow through us. God then can use us to bring life to others because he is having his way in our lives.

Squelching Inner Renewal

I often must choose God's will over my own. One of the more difficult choices I must make—and I have had to make it repeatedly—is to continue traveling from city to city and country to country to preach the gospel. It's a battle. Many times I would rather stay at home. Yet I know I must make the right choice. When I choose God's will over my will, I know that the death of Jesus is at work in me and the life of Jesus is going to flow through me. I know that God is going to use me to do something for his glory because he is having his way in my life.

I know an evangelical pastor in southern Mexico God used in an unusual way. This pastor had been persecuted for his beliefs, but one day he received a telegram from one of the men who had opposed him. To his surprise, it read, "Dear Pastor: I urgently need to see you. Please fly to my village immediately. The only way to get here is by small plane. We have a little landing strip."

"Who does this guy think he is?" the pastor exclaimed to his wife. "He isn't going to give me orders! If he wants to see me, he'll have to come to me. Besides, I don't have the money to rent a plane." But for three days, this pastor couldn't rest. He couldn't pray or read his Bible in peace. Finally, he decided to scrape the money together, rent a plane, and visit the man.

It wasn't easy to find the village in the mountainous jungle. But when the pastor landed, the man who had sent the telegram was there to greet them. "Brother," the man said, "I'm so glad you're here!"

Brother? the pastor thought. *I'm not so sure we're brothers.* But he politely asked, "Why did you send for me?"

"Well," the man explained, "about five years ago I had a leadership position in a church in Veracruz. I began to read the New Testament and was born again. I started preaching the Bible and many people in my church became Christians. Then I was sent to this little village, and I've been preaching the same message here. Now nearly everyone in this village is a Christian."

"That's wonderful," the surprised pastor said, "but I still don't know why you needed me."

"We want you to baptize us," the man answered, "and I want to be first."

So the pastor baptized every believer in a river that ran through the village. He witnessed their joy and was greatly blessed. Had that pastor continued to resist God's will in this seemingly unimportant matter, he would have missed a great blessing. Yet he chose God's will over his own—and was rewarded.

Sometimes we think the choices we have to make between our will and God's will are insignificant. We think, *Oh, this decision isn't that important. It won't matter if I choose my will instead of God's will this time.* But that is not the case. Every time we choose God's will over our own, the life of Jesus flows through us. When we choose our will instead of God's will, we are refusing the death of Jesus. We are refusing to carry the cross. We are refusing to die like a grain of wheat so that we may bear fruit. We miss the blessing of the life of Jesus flowing through us and cause others to miss that blessing, too.

Several years ago I had the opportunity to share the gospel with the president of the Dominican Republic. Our evangelistic team was in Santo Domingo for a crusade, and we invited the key people of the city, including the president, to a breakfast. He did not attend, but sent a lawyer to represent him. As I spoke with this lawyer, she said, "The president would like to meet you before you leave the country. But he can see you only on Sunday, immediately after mass, in the chapel of the presidential palace. If you come to mass with him, he will have forty-five minutes to talk with you. His chauffeur will pick you up at 8:30 Sunday morning."

"I'll be there!" I said. As far as I knew, no one ever had witnessed to this man before. What an exciting opportunity!

After my initial excitement wore off, though, I began to worry. *Some non-Catholic Christians might hear about me sitting through mass and become upset with me,* I thought. *I can't go through with this.* I talked with some pastors in Santo Domingo who confirmed my fear. They told me I'd better not go. Then I consulted a Christian lawyer who worked closely with the government; he told me I should go to mass and witness to the president. I knew what the Lord would have me do—but I turned coward.

When the chauffeur arrived, I sent him away.

Was I discouraged afterward! My joy was gone. That afternoon, I prayed, "Lord, forgive me. I'll never turn down an opportunity to witness to somebody because I fear what others might think." The Lord forgave me and gave me relief about this incident, but I learned that the life of Jesus cannot flow through me to others if I choose my will over his.

Older Christians sometimes face a danger in this area. They may suddenly stop choosing God's will over their own. They may think, like David did when he committed adultery with Bathsheba, *I've been serving the Lord faithfully for more than twenty years. It's time for me to take it easy for a while. It's not going to hurt to do things my way.* But living for Christ is not something we decide to do just for a time. We must continually decide to choose God's will over our own.

Whenever we knowingly refuse God's will, we are saddled with defeat, discouragement, and depression. We cannot be filled with the joy of the Spirit. We miss out on the opportunities and blessings God wants to bestow upon us. But if we confess our sins—if we confess the times we have chosen our will rather than God's—he will cleanse, purify, and use us.

Sharing the Life of Jesus

One characteristic of believers who walk with the indwelling Christ is that they find ways to share their knowledge of the Savior. They don't have to be kicked, shoved, pushed, or cajoled into witnessing. They don't have to be harangued by a minister or carry on in grim determination. They don't need courses on how to evangelize others (although there's nothing wrong with such courses). A believer filled with the indwelling Christ will find ways to share the gospel according to his temperament, talents, education—all under the Holy Spirit's guidance.

Paul describes this phenomenon:

It is written: "I believed; therefore I have spoken." With that same spirit of faith we also believe and therefore speak, because we know that the one who raised the Lord Jesus from the dead will also raise us with Jesus and present us with you in his presence. All this is for your benefit, so that the grace that is reaching more and more people may cause thanksgiving to overflow to the glory of God (2 Cor. 4:13-15).

We speak because we believe. We don't speak because we're brilliant. We don't speak because someone told us to. We don't speak to alleviate our guilt. We speak because we believe. We're so excited about what we've found in Christ that we want to share it with others. We speak because God makes us capable of loving others and sharing the Good News with them.

God can use any human being for his glory, no matter how little ability, charisma, or knowledge that person may possess. Ordinary people have spoken out of their belief, and God has used them to open whole countries to the gospel. One of these people is my friend, Dave Farah, who was a Wycliffe missionary to Bolivia.

After working as an administrator of Wycliffe's Jungle Center in Bolivia for eight years, Dave was asked to move to La Paz, the capital city, to take over the responsibility of government relations. Shortly afterward he contacted the minister of education, a military colonel. Dave started to pray for this man, asking the Lord for an opportunity to witness to him.

Before long, a revolution took place and the colonel disappeared. Revolutions are nothing new in South America. Bolivia has averaged more than one revolution a year for the past 160 years. But Dave had a bad feeling about the colonel's disappearance. No one knew where he was. So Dave prayed for an opportunity to help him.

One day a newspaper reported that the colonel had sought refuge in the Argentine embassy. When Dave learned of this, he prayed for a way to contact the colonel. He wanted to try to get a New Testament to him. Dave underlined verses in the Spanish New Testament, enclosed a letter explaining the way of salvation, and gave it to the guard at the Argentine embassy, asking him to give it to the colonel. Dave walked away, not knowing whether his request would be honored.

Later, the colonel telephoned Dave and said, "You were the only person who contacted me while I was in hiding. My friends ignored me. I had nothing else to do, so I read the New Testament."

Soon another revolution took place and the colonel became president of Bolivia. Shortly after the inauguration, Dave telephoned the colonel and asked to see him. The colonel immediately set up an appointment, greeting Dave like an old friend, and gave him a big hug (as we Latins do).

"What can I do for you?" the colonel asked, expecting Dave to ask a favor.

"Nothing," Dave replied. "I just want to pray for you, your family, your government, and Bolivia."

"No one has ever prayed for me before," the colonel said in amazement. "Please, pray for me."

So Dave prayed. When he finished, the colonel was crying.

Before long, Dave invited the colonel to accompany him on a vacation. "Wycliffe has a house in the jungle where it's nice and warm. Let's go down there to relax and enjoy some fishing."

During their vacation, Dave and the colonel talked about many things, including corruption and lack of trust in the government. When Dave said the country needed a moral revival, the colonel became excited and asked Dave to draw up a plan for a morality campaign in Bolivia.

Part of the plan included Bolivia's first presidential prayer breakfast, at which I was invited to speak. During this breakfast I had an intimate conversation with the colonel. He opened his heart and shared his deepest concerns with me. Here was a man who had the same personal and family problems as all the rest of us, plus the worries of governing more than six million people. As we talked, I was able to explain God's plan of salvation to him. It took him a while to believe that God would forgive him for some of the things he had done, but before we parted he received Christ as his Savior.

Grateful for his new relationship with Christ, the colonel asked, "Luis, what can I do for you while you're in Bolivia?"

"Well," I replied, "our crusade is scheduled to run for five days. It would be fantastic if we could be on national television during that time."

The colonel immediately told an aide to put our program on the national network for five nights. "What time would be best for you?" he asked.

"Ten to eleven in the evening," I said.

"Fine. You have five nights from ten to eleven."

What an exciting opportunity! But there's more. We received three thousand *Living New Testaments* from the World Home Bible League to offer free during the television program. We gave all three thousand away.

When the colonel saw that we were giving New Testaments to the people, he decided that all the religious education classes in Bolivia should be based on the New Testament. With the help of the World Home Bible League, Dave offered the government a million copies of the *Living New Testament*. They since have been used in religious education classes throughout Bolivia and have played a significant role in the spiritual awakening of that country.

This great work was not the result of a single, momentous decision, but of one man continuously obeying God in little things—praying for a military officer, sending a New Testament to someone in need, extending to him genuine care and friendship.

When we believe that the life of Jesus is at work within us, we will share the Good News with others. We may stumble along the way, we may make mistakes, but we will communicate. Sometimes we make the mistake of thinking, *If I were not so plain, I could be a great soul winner. If I were a more dynamic speaker, people would listen to me.* But the secret is not in what we look like but in the treasure at work within us whenever we choose God's will over our own.

Living in Daily Renewal

The power of the indwelling Christ is what keeps dynamic Christians excited about life. The preeminent characteristic of God's outstanding servants throughout church history is that, with few exceptions, they persistently served the Lord. John Wesley and Corrie ten Boom immediately come to mind. Both served God long after the age most people hope to retire. They weren't persistent out of their own stubbornness, like many unhappy Christians who strive to serve God out of their own ability.

Rather, these servants persistently walked in the power of the indwelling Christ. This gave them freedom from worry about their mistakes, problems, and weaknesses.

As we walk in the power of the indwelling Christ, eternity's values become more important to us. Lost people become our obsession because lost people are God's obsession. Although we still hold jobs, earn a living, and pay bills, these things no longer are the focus of our lives. Although we work to keep ourselves attractive, we are not preoccupied with clothes, hairstyles, or shoes. Our primary purpose and source of excitement is to reach out to the lost.

I am concerned about the number of Christians who live imbalanced lives, who seek the excitement and thrills of ego-centered activities. Our greatest kicks in life should not come from the plastic excitement of new cars, houses, or the latest vacation spots. The excitement of seeing the living Christ transform people is where real excitement is to be found.

When the life of Jesus is at work within us, enabling us to communicate the gospel naturally as we go through life, we will be renewed day by day. Spiritual renewal isn't a movement. It occurs daily when we walk in God's will again and again and again.

One of the exciting things about spiritual renewal is that the older we are and the longer we walk with Christ, the more renewed and youthful we become. As Paul says, "Though outwardly we are wasting away, yet inwardly we are being renewed day by day" (2 Cor. 4:16). What a thrill! When we walk with Christ, our bodies may weaken and fall apart, but spiritually we are growing stronger every day. Can you imagine how "super-renewed" you will be after choosing God's will over your will for fifty, sixty, or seventy years? Your old body may fall apart, but the inner person is just beginning to show through.

Several years ago I sat next to Joy Ridderhof of Gospel Recordings at a fund-raising dinner. She had been a missionary in Latin America and talked to me at machine-gun pace, in Spanish, all through dinner. Though Joy was in her seventies at the time, she didn't talk about the old days. Instead, she talked about my ministry. She talked of how we could enhance our follow-up of new believers by giving them a recording of some of my messages on Christian growth.

I told her she had a good idea, but I didn't see how our team could afford to pay for such a venture. "Don't worry about the money, Luis," she replied. "Just record some messages and send them to me right away."

When I arrived home several days later, I received a letter from Joy reminding me that I needed to send her the messages. I did, and she provided our team with thousands of records to give to new Christians. When I'm in my seventies, that's the kind of vision and faith I want to have!

When we are renewed through Jesus Christ, the excitement never dies. We don't lose heart!

The life of Jesus just flows stronger and stronger, renewing us more and more. We are joyful and victorious because the Lord Jesus is alive and working within us. This is what Christianity is all about. It isn't a religion we follow—it's the life of Christ that fills us, making us new people.

Luis Palau is an international evangelist who has preached the gospel to more than nine million people on six continents, and to millions more through radio and television broadcasts in ninety-five countries. He is author of thirty-one books and booklets. Dr. Palau and his wife, Pat, live in Portland, Oregon, near the international headquarters of the Luis Palau Evangelistic Association.

To correspond with the author, please write to:

Luis Palau
EVANGELISTIC ASSOCIATION

International Headquarters
Post Office Box 1173
Portland, OR 97207-1173
United States

Want More? . . .
Say Yes!

Has this booklet whet your appetite for personal renewal? Would you appreciate some additional practical ideas and suggestions for capturing or maintaining your passion for spiritual things? Would you like to bring this message of renewal to your Bible study group or congregation?

Say Yes! by Luis Palau is the book for you. Walk with Luis on his own journey of spiritual renewal. Share in his passion for spiritual things. Practical advice and heart-felt stories make this 168 page paperback an invigorating study. Pick up copies for you and a friend at your local Christian bookstore.